WALKS FOR ALL AGES
CAMBRIDGESHIRE

WALKS FOR ALL AGES

CAMBRIDGESHIRE

CLIVE BROWN

BRADWELL
BOOKS

Published by Bradwell Books
9 Orgreave Close Sheffield S13 9NP
Email: books@bradwellbooks.co.uk

British Library Cataloguing in Publication Data: a catalogue record for this book is available from the British Library.

1st Edition

ISBN: 9781909914902

Print: Gomer Press, Llandysul, Ceredigion SA44 4JL

Design by: Erik Siewko Creative, Derbyshire.
eriksiewko@gmail.com

Photograph Credits: © Clive Brown
and credited seperately where applicable.
Front cover © National Trust Images / Robert Morris

Maps: Contain Ordnance Survey data
© Crown copyright and database right 2015

Ordnance Survey licence number 100039353

The information in this book has been produced in good faith and is intended as a general guide. Bradwell Books and its authors have made all reasonable efforts to ensure that the details are correct at the time of publication. Bradwell Books and the author cannot accept any responsibility for any changes that have taken place subsequent to the book being published. It is the responsibility of individuals undertaking any of the walks listed in this publication to exercise due care and consideration for the health and wellbeing of each other in the party. Particular care should be taken if you are inexperienced. The walks in this book are not especially strenuous but individuals taking part should ensure they are fit and able to complete the walk before setting off.

WALKS FOR ALL AGES

INTRODUCTION

Cambridgeshire is a county of contrasts; from the flat fenland in the north and north-east to the undulating higher ground in the south and west; from the highbrow university environments to the hard-working farm employees tilling the soil and growing food for the nation.

A county of brash and confident young companies churning out complex software and ground-breaking new technological marvels, to long-established organisations manufacturing traditional items like bricks and building materials.

Flat reclaimed fenland is interlaced with unseen ditches; totally silent one day apart from a passing car or a contented bird singing in the bulrushes, it will the next day be host to a giant tractor going up and down the fields with its engine shattering the silence with a loud roar.

The colours of the fields in Cambridgeshire during the modern farming year range from several tones of dark brown straight after ploughing into the myriad shades of green of the growing crops and the conspicuous yellow of the now abundant rapeseed to the lighter browns and khakis of crops ready to harvest.

The county has a long history of involvement in the aviation industry and one is never very far away from a disused Second World War airfield. The cemetery at Madingley is testament to the huge local presence of American airmen during World War II; it contains the graves of nearly four thousand American servicemen and a memorial to over five thousand more.

Unsuspecting travellers along Newmarket Road are still surprised to be held up by traffic lights as a massive jumbo jet passes low on its manoeuvre in or out of Cambridge Airport. Maintenance of a wide range of aircraft and constant training sessions keep the airport busy. Over at the airfield at Duxford, the former Battle of Britain and later USAAF airfield has one of the best collections of historic aircraft in this country.

The Great Ouse and Cam rivers dominate the county. The source of the Great Ouse is near Syresham on the borders of Northamptonshire and Bedfordshire. The river runs in a generally north-east direction to the Wash at King's Lynn, and is joined by its major tributary, the Cam at Popes Corner, south of Ely. The waters of the Cam flow from the south to Cambridge under a confusing number of names, including the Rhee, the Granta and the Linton Cam, which is also sometimes confusingly known as the Bourn River.

BAITS BITE LOCK

Twice a year during Lent and then May Week (which happens in June), the river from Baits Bite Lock to Chesterton is the location of the Cambridge Bumps.

There are ten races each day over four days each with 17 to 18 boats lining up about one-and-a-half lengths apart. A cannon is fired to start the race and the objective is to catch the boat in front and either overtake it, or 'bump' it by touching any part of it, although hard collisions are discouraged. Any crew managing a bump moves up a place in the next day's start. The rules are quite complicated to an outsider. When a bump occurs, the two boats drop out of the racing; if a boat then overtakes the boat in front of them now (three places ahead) it has moved up the order faster by what is called an overbump. The aim of each crew is to move up four places over the four days of the competition. The finishing order at the end of the last day is the starting order for the next year. The crew finishing at the top of the standings is acknowledged as 'Head of the River'.

Horningsea existed as a Roman settlement; pottery was manufactured here from the 2nd to the 4th century (CE). Broken pottery is still easily found in fields and gardens in the village. The village sign, a man in peasant clothing working at a treadle-operated potter's wheel, reflects this.

Car Dyke, which joins the River Cam here, is the route of a Roman canal, running for 85 miles (140km) from Lincoln to Cambridge, via Peterborough. The view that is was a canal was first promoted by an 18th-century archaeologist, but some historians disagree and say that it can only have been built for drainage. One of the problems the Romans would have had to overcome is that there are several changes of level between the three cities, and locks – even rudimentary single-gate flash locks – were not used in this country for another thousand years. There are good arguments each way, but modern opinions are that it was probably a boundary ditch also used for drainage that was useful for transportation in some locations.

THE BASICS

Distance: 4½ miles / 7.2km

Gradient: Flat

Severity: Easy

Approx. time to walk: 2 hrs

Stiles: None

Maps: OS Landranger 154 (Cambridge & Newmarket); Explorer 226 (Ely & Newmarket); there is one very short section on Explorer 209 (Cambridge)

Path description: Hard surfaced paths, grassy fields; two short field sections

Start point: The bridge over the River Cam at Clayhithe (GR TL 501644)

Parking: Small roadside hard standing on the road to Waterbeach (CB25 9HZ)

Dog friendly: Yes; they would be best on a lead along the roadside paths

Public toilets: None

Nearest food: The Bridge pub at the start/finish, other pubs and a café in Waterbeach

BAITS BITE LOCK WALK

1. Take the path to the river and turn right along the towpath with the river to the left for 2 miles (3km) to Baits Bite Lock and cross the river by the footbridges.

2. Follow the path right of the house and keep ahead on the wide track bearing left. As this track swings right keep straight on, over the footbridge, up the narrower path with the trees to the left, all the way to the road.

3. Turn left along the roadside path, through Horningsea and out of the village; continue along the wide grass verge to the layby and the signpost for Clayhithe.

4. Bear right to the signpost close by and cross the field ahead, again signposted to Clayhithe; this field may be under cultivation but a track should be well marked within any crops. Carry on over the next field which may again be under cultivation, to the kissing gate. Bear right; there should be a noticeable track in the grass, through the midway gate, to the kissing gate at the far right corner.

5. Go through and take the wide farm road, left/straight on. As this road swings right, keep straight on along the grassy track between fields, past the marker post by the large tree in the boundary and straight on across the next field (which may be under cultivation) to the marker post at a crossroads with a stony farm road.

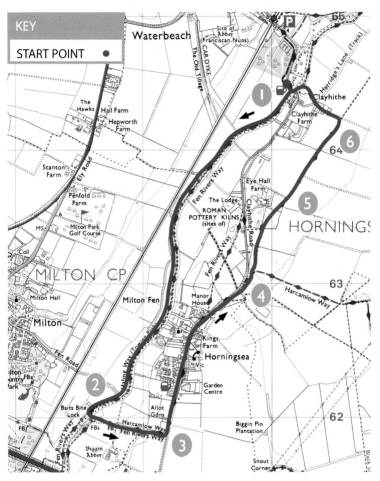

KEY

START POINT ●

6. Take this road left, between farm buildings to the crossroads with the tarmac road; keep ahead bearing right of the tall hedge and a marker post, then left to the river and the road. Cross carefully and turn right over the bridge. Take the path back to the parking area.

BOTTISHAM LODE

BOTTISHAM LODE, 2.5 MILES (4KM) LONG, RUNS IN AN ALMOST STRAIGHT LINE FROM THE RIVER CAM NEAR BOTTISHAM LOCK TO THE VILLAGE OF LODE.

The waterway is fed by Quy Water, but neither goes particularly close to the village of Bottisham. The lode was used regularly by smaller commercial boats during the late 17th to 19th centuries, but volumes of trade fell with the arrival of the railways and traffic ceased about 1900. There is also evidence that boats once used Quy Water but neither has been navigable for some years.

The Conservators of the River Cam is the Navigation Authority on the Cam between Bottisham Lock and the Mill Pond. It is an organisation created in 1702, authorised to charge tolls so that it can improve the river. The organisation, run by a board of thirteen Conservators, built the house in Clayhithe in 1842 at a cost of £880. They looked after their own interests by including a large room for meetings and banquets.

Waterbeach has some evidence of Roman settlement; the Car Dyke canal passed the edge of the village to join the River Cam close by. Both Waterbeach and Landbeach were known as Beche or Beck during the Dark Ages; this became Utbech in the Norman Domesday Book. Architecturally it looks like any other fenland large village/small town; its position close on the A10 and next to a busy railway line make it an ideal dormitory settlement for Cambridge and for London.

RAF Waterbeach was built in 1940; in the latter part of World War II 514 Squadron were based here, operating Avro Lancaster bombers. They flew 218 raids, dropping nearly 15,000 tons of bombs on Germany and military infrastructure in France. The station became part of Fighter Command all through the 1950s with various jet fighters including the Gloster Meteor and Hawker Hunter based there. The RAF left in the mid-60s and from then until 2012 it was used by the Army as a base for part of the Royal Engineers. The base has now been closed and has been earmarked for new housing.

THE BASICS

Distance: 3½ miles / 5.6km

Gradient: Flat, with short climbs only to the top of embankments

Severity: Easy

Approx. time to walk: 1½ hrs

Stiles: Four (not dog friendly)

Maps: OS Landranger 154 (Cambridge & Newmarket); Explorer 226 (Ely & Newmarket)

Path description: Riverside embankments, hard paths, a grassy field

Start point: The bridge over the River Cam at Clayhithe, south-east of Waterbeach. (GR TL 501644)

Parking: Small roadside hard standing on the road to Waterbeach (CB25 9HZ)

Dog friendly: Four stiles, but not adapted for dogs

Public toilets: None

Nearest food: The Bridge pub at the start

BOTTISHAM LODE WALK

1. Take the path from the back of the parking area to the river; turn left, up to the road and cross the bridge to the right. Turn left, signposted Upware, along the riverbank to the signpost and turn right up the track passing left of the River Cam Conservancy shed. Continue between the barns to the marker post.

2. Turn left, across the field which may be under cultivation. A track should, however, be visible within any crop. Carry on through the wide gap ahead and the tarmac drive all the way to the junction. Turn right and left, around the farmhouse to the stile; cross and keep ahead with the fence to the left over the next stile. Continue to the stile in the hedge gap at the far left corner.

3. Cross and turn left, through this wide field with the Bottisham Lode to the right; over the stile at the boundary along the embankment with the lode still right, through the kissing gate to the river by the white bridge. The simple utilitarian building at the end of the lode on the banks of the Cam is a pump house to raise the water from the lode into the river.

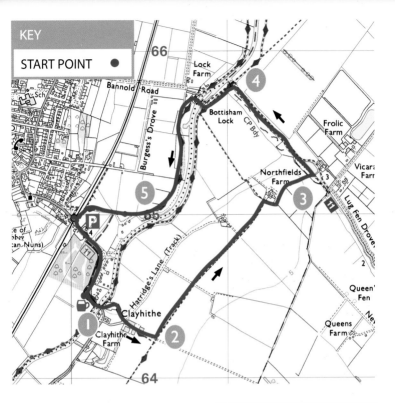

4.   Turn left and cross the river at Bottisham Lock, follow the path right and turn left with the fence, through a gate and along the top of the embankment with the river now on the left.

5.   The river veers right and the path goes further right, down to a gate. Go through and follow the path between the hedge and the embankment. The path leads to the top of the embankment, through a kissing gate and a gate close to the station. Turn left through the gate at the road and cross next to the level crossing. Take the path left back to the parking area.

BUFF WOOD

Buff Wood has been a Site of Special Scientific Interest (SSSI) for nearly fifty years since 1958. It is regarded as one of the richest boulder clay woodlands in Cambridgeshire. SSSIs were first designated under the National Parks and Access to the Countryside Act of 1949.

The Hatleys, Hatley St George and East Hatley were historically separate parishes until joined together in 1957. Between the Hatley villages and the B1046 lies Hayley Wood, whose name is too close surely for it not to be a derivative of Hatley? A large wood was mentioned in this area in the Domesday Book, but the oak trees in the wood date from 1780 to 1840; this wood is also an SSSI.

Hatley Park is privately owned. During the Civil War it belonged to Sir George Downing, a Cromwell supporter who switched sides to back Charles II after the Restoration. He dabbled in London property and developed Downing Street in the 1680s. His grandson, also Sir George, died without heirs and left his fortune to found Downing College in Cambridge. The college owned Hatley Park until 1947.

In the latter part of the 20th century it was owned by John Jacob Astor VII, the politician, agricultural expert and horse racing executive. He was the son of Lady Astor, the first woman to take her seat in the House of Commons, and was named after his relative John Jacob Astor IV who died on the Titanic.

THE BASICS

Distance: 4¾ miles / 7.7km

Gradient: One easy slope uphill

Severity: Easy

Approx. time to walk: 2½ hrs

Stiles: None

Maps: OS Landranger 153 (Bedford and Huntingdon); Explorer 208 (Bedford and St Neots)

Path description: Grassy field edges, hard paths and wider hardcore farm roads

Start point: The Post Office, 6 Main Road, Hatley St George. (GR TL 282509)

Parking: Considerate roadside parking, or there is a small parking area at the village hall; check if this is OK; limited bus service, Thursdays only (SG19 3HW)

Dog friendly: Yes

Public toilets: None

Nearest food: The Crown and Cushion in the Great Gransden or the Cock Inn and the Wheatsheaf in Gamblingay; check opening hours

BUFF WOOD WALK

1. Facing away from the Post Office turn right, to the bridleway signpost on the left. Turn right up the hedged track; keep your direction on the farm road on the left-hand field edge with the hedge to the left, to the marker post on the left. Turn left up this farm road on the field edge with the hedge to the right, to the water recycling plant. Turn right through the gap and immediately left in the original direction hedge again to the left, bearing right to the marker post in the hedge gap.

2. Turn left through the wide gateway and continue direction back to the road. Go through the gate here and turn right, along the road to the signpost at the wide metal gate on the left.

3. Go through the gate and follow the track in the grass ahead, across the road and over the cattle grid. Continue between farm buildings and then trees on a less substantial but still wide estate road; keep ahead on the track on the field edge with the trees to the right. This main hard track swings left at a marker

post, keep direction up the wide track between trees and re-join the field edge. Maintain direction, keeping the trees to the right. This track is called Bar Lane and forms the boundary between Cambridgeshire to the left and Bedfordshire to the right. Carry on with the trees right to where the lane ends at a T-junction of tracks just beyond three marker posts.

4. Turn left and follow the path through the narrow gap, and continue ahead with the hedge to the left, bearing right to a narrow gap on the left.

5. Go through and take this field edge with the hedge and trees to the left for two-thirds of a mile (1km); the track bears slightly right to a narrow gap on the left.

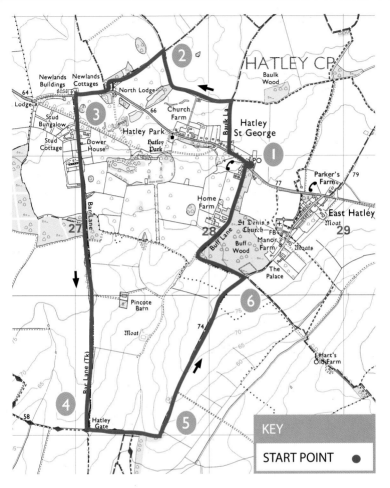

KEY

START POINT ●

6. Turn left, passing left of the brick barn; carry on downslope on the track on the right-hand field edge with Buff Wood to the right. Turn right at the corner of the wood; this farm road, Buff Lane, leads ahead past Home Farm to the road in Hatley St George and the Post Office.

CAMBRIDGE COLLEGES

Cambridge ranks as one of the most fascinating cities in this country, and there is always something new and interesting around each corner.

The castle in Cambridge was built from 1068 and the first town charter was granted by Henry III at the beginning of the 12th century. The area had been settled since the end of the Iron Age, with Romans, Saxons and Vikings all living and trading locally. Cambridge did not, however, become a city until 1951; it has no cathedral and is part of Ely Diocese. The university was founded in 1209 by students and teachers escaping from the regular 'town and gown' riots in Oxford when several students were killed. The subsequent loss of trade soon convinced the residents to persuade the refugees back, but some stayed and the new seat of learning

thrived. The oldest surviving college is Peterhouse, founded in 1284.

The Walk

1. Take the path bearing right away from the toilets, across Christ's Pieces, past the fenced bowling green to Emmanuel Road and bear left along the roadside path. Go past the Methodist Church to the roundabout and keep straight on along Victoria Avenue.

2. As the railings around Jesus College end, bear left on the tarmac path between the avenue of trees all the way to Jesus Lock. The river downstream from Jesus Lock is known as the Lower River, from the lock to the Mill Pond and sluice (just beyond Silver Street Bridge) is the Middle River and the Upper River is beyond. Motorised craft are not allowed on the Middle and Upper River in summer (April to September), so this section is always crowded with punts.

3. Turn left along the path with the river to the right and continue on the boardwalk next to the river up to the road at Magdalene Bridge. Magdalene Bridge (pronounced Maudlin; the college is close by) is believed to be the site of the Roman ford across the Cam

and the location of the first bridge, built by the Saxons in the 8th century. Turn right, over the bridge and up the road to the traffic lights at the crossroads.

4. The route goes left on Northampton Street and left at the mini-roundabout along Queen's Road. Bear left to the Trinity Metal gates and right on a hardcore path between trees with the dyke to the left. The area of grass between the road and the river is known as The Backs. The stunning architectural gem, King's College Chapel, was begun in 1446 when the foundation stone was laid by King Henry VI. Building continued through the turbulence of the Wars of the Roses and the reign of King Henry VII to its completion in 1515. Work continued on finishing the windows for some years longer. Continue on this path bearing left around the semi-circular Queen's College to Silver Street Bridge.

THE BASICS

Distance: 4 miles / 6.5km

Gradient: Flat

Severity: Easy

Approx. time to walk: 2 hrs, but allow longer for sightseeing

Stiles: None

Maps: OS Landranger 154 (Cambridge & Newmarket); Explorer 209 (Cambridge)

Path description: City streets, roadside paths, tarmac paths and a hard path along The Backs

Start point: The bus station in Cambridge. (GR TL 452584)

Parking: Any Cambridge city centre car park (CB2 3BZ)

Dog friendly: Yes. Dogs will need to be on a lead in the city streets

Public toilets: On site and plenty more in the city centre

Nearest food: Loads of possibilities in the city and on the route

5. On the left can be seen the Mathematical Bridge, into another part of Queen's. Extensive records still exist detailing the costs of construction of the bridge. The designer of the bridge, William Etheridge, received a fee of £21 which included the supply of a model of the bridge still possessed by the college. The myth that the bridge was first built without any nails or bolts was probably begun because none could be seen from the bridge decking. The entire structure had to be replaced in 1905, with the timbers being bolted together. Carry on over the bridge and turn right down the alleyway Laundress Lane.

6. Cross the cobbled bridge to the right, go through the barrier and turn left along the wide tarmac path with the river to the left. Keep ahead past the sluice and across the canoe rollers all the way to the road at Fen Causeway. Turn left, along to the traffic lights at the junction.

7. Take the roadside path left. Across the road is a memorial to the people involved in the creation of Hobson's Conduit. The conduit was dug between 1610 and 1614 to supply fresh water to the citizens of Cambridge. Water still travels along some of the roadside conduits under the control of the council's drainage engineer. Several prominent Cambridge men were involved in the construction of the waterway but Thomas Hobson endowed a Hobson's Conduit Trust and the name has stuck. This is the same Hobson who used to operate a livery stable in the city. He found that all his best horses were taken first and consequently were always tired and worn out. He started a system where when you hired a horse, you had to take the one he offered or none at all, giving rise to the term 'Hobson's Choice'. Keep straight on to the Fitzwilliam Museum.

8. The Fitzwilliam Museum has nearly half a million visitors per year. It opened in 1816 with a bequest of the library and art collection of Viscount Fitzwilliam. It moved into the present building in 1848. Continue your direction, passing left of St Bene't's Church; the name is a contraction of Benedict. The church is thought to be the oldest building in Cambridge, with the tower having been built in the early years of the 11th century. Do not miss the Corpus Clock, facing slightly away from the direction of travel at the corner of Trumpington Street and Bene't Street, in the corner of the Taylor Library building. It is a mechanical clock, installed in 2008, showing the time in blue LEDs shining through slits in the face of the clock. Carry on past the other end of King's College Chapel and ahead on the wider thoroughfare with Great St Mary's Church to the right. Notice the clock above the doorway.

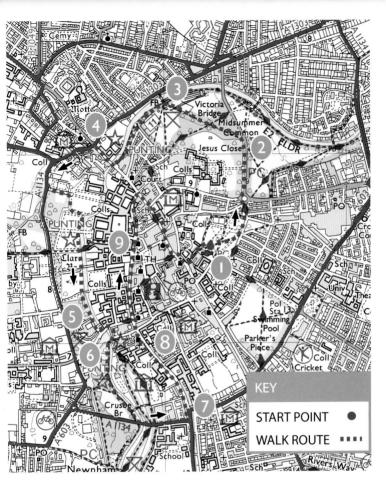

9. The route goes ahead slightly right, up Trinity Street; bearing right on St John's Street, to the junction with the Round Church across the road. The Church of the Holy Sepulchre is one of only four remaining historic round churches in England. The building dates from 1130, probably inspired by the rotunda of the Church of the Holy Sepulchre in Jerusalem; it was built as a chapel for pilgrims on the Via Devana. Turn right and follow Sidney Street to the Church of St Andrew the Great, bear slight left and right as Hobson Street joins from the left. Take pedestrianised Christ's Lane to the left and turn right to the bus station and the starting point.

GODMANCHESTER

THE CHINESE BRIDGE IN GODMANCHESTER SHARES AN APOCRYPHAL TALE WITH THE MATHEMATICAL BRIDGE IN CAMBRIDGE. THE COMMON BELIEF IS THAT THEY WERE FIRST BUILT WITHOUT BOLTS OR NAILS AND THEN DISMANTLED BY ARCHITECTURAL EXPERTS TO SEE HOW IT WAS DONE. THE EXPERTS WERE THEN UNABLE TO REASSEMBLE THEM AND BOLTS AND NAILS HAD TO BE USED.

This is unlikely, looking at the design of the Chinese Bridge and its fairly well-documented history. The first bridge was built in 1827, probably inspired by a bridge in the Chinese Chippendale style just downstream, connecting Island Hall with an ornamental island. The bridge deteriorated and had to be replaced by a replica in 1960; this replica had to be replaced itself by a second replica in 2010.

Godmanchester has been settled for over 2,000 years. The Roman town that developed around the mansio or travellers' inn, at the crossroads of the Colchester to Chester Via Devana and the London to York Ermine Street, was built on the site of an earlier Iron Age village.

Godmanchester's buildings reflect a cross-section of houses across the centuries, from almost pre-medieval wattle and daub cottages, through Tudor wood frame and 18th-century gentlemen's residences, thirties semis, fifties ex-council properties and sprawling new seventies-to-nineties housing estates.

The site of Huntingdon Castle is believed to have been occupied as a strong point by Viking settlers until they were ousted as part of the reunification of the Danelaw by Alfred the Great's son, Edward the Elder. William the Conqueror built a castle here in 1068, which saw military action during the Civil War between Matilda and King Stephen. Further hostilities took place later in the century, when Prince Henry, the oldest son of Henry II, led a rebellion against his father. A siege of Huntingdon Castle was not lifted until the appearance of Henry himself in 1174; he later ordered the castle's demolition.

Historians are not sure how far the destruction went as the castle was in use again during the Civil War, after which it did gradually fall into dereliction. A windmill stood on the castle mound for most of the 19th century; this was removed in 1875 and the castle remains a plain grassy mound.

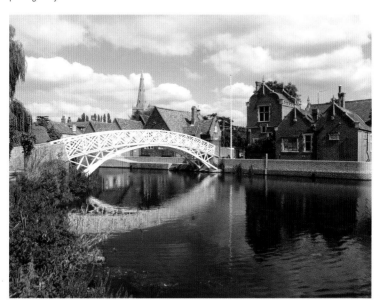

THE BASICS

Distance: 4¼ miles / 7km

Gradient: Mainly flat, slight slopes up or down embankments only

Severity: Easy

Approx. time to walk: 2¼ hrs

Stiles: Three

Maps: OS Landranger 153 (Bedford & Huntingdon); Explorer 225 (Huntingdon & St Ives)

Path description: Tarmac paths, hard surfaced tracks and grassy paths

Start point: The small parking area at the Old Town Hall, Post Street, Godmanchester (GR TL 244706)

Parking: Any car park in the town (PE29 2NB)

Dog friendly: No, there are several stiles and they will need to be on a lead next to the busier roads

Public toilets: At the start

Nearest food: Loads of possibilities in the town

GODMANCHESTER WALK

1. Take Post Road towards Huntingdon, along the left-hand roadside path, then carry on under the A14 flyover and over the footbridge next to the old bridge across the Great Ouse. The medieval bridge here connecting Godmanchester to Huntingdon is believed to have been built in 1332. The method of building from both ends to meet in the middle is confirmed by the slight kink in the centre and the fact that the pedestrian refuges are a different shape in the northern half to the southern half. A pedestrian footbridge and the modern bypass, now the A14, opened in 1975, meaning that the bridge now carries only local traffic. Continue past the Old Bridge hotel to the traffic lights.

2. Turn left along the path right of the castle mound bearing right with the trees to the right. Exit along the path from the right-hand corner to the road at a car park. Turn left back under the A14 and immediate right at the signpost up Mill Common to the signpost on the left.

3. Turn left down the gravel drive and over the bridge at Garkie's Mill Small Sluice; turn right past another sluice and along the path through trees between branches of the river, bearing left over open land into the trees at the far left. Go up the steps and over the substantial footbridge.

4. Turn right, then left along the field edge next to the trees at the bottom of the railway embankment, to the far right corner. The railway here is the East Coast Main Line from London to Edinburgh, a relative latecomer in the development of railway travel; this line did not open until 1850. The corresponding West Coast Main Line to the industrial north and north-west had been built during the late 1830s. Carry on through the fence and step over the stile.

5. Take the track left over the bridge and through the kissing gate. The meadow ahead is Portholme and is the largest meadow in England at 257 acres or about 1km². The meadow area was once used for horse racing until the opening of the purpose-built racecourse near the Great North Road in late Victorian times. The large flat area was also popular with early aviators. James Radley first landed here in 1910 in a Bleriot monoplane. A series of flying exhibitions followed until the beginning of the First World War

KEY

START POINT ●

when the area was used by the Royal Flying Corps. It was last used by Alan Cobham's Flying Circus in the 1930s. Keep direction in a straight line (there is normally a track in the grass) across Portholme to Godmanchester Lock.

6. Cross the footbridge and take the path left, with the river to the right, leading round to the Chinese Bridge. Cross this bridge and go through the car park to the Old Town Hall in the town centre.

DEVIL'S DYKE

THERE IS STILL AN AIR OF MYSTERY ABOUT DEVIL'S DYKE. EVEN
IN MODERN TIMES NO ONE IS VERY SURE WHEN OR WHY IT WAS
BUILT.

The Dyke, the largest of several similar Cambridgeshire earthworks, is up to 30 feet (9m) high and runs in a straight line from the village of Reach on the edge of the fens for 7½ miles (12km) to Woodditton. It crossed Roman roads so would appear to have been built after the occupation and was mentioned in the Anglo-Saxon Chronicle and other important documents. Recent archaeological research puts the date of construction at around the 5th to 6th century. The dyke could be a defensive measure between the Mercian and East Anglian Kingdoms. Solitary travellers and small groups of people would have no problem negotiating the thick woodland to the south of the dyke or the village and Lode at the northern end. It would be a different story for a large army or raiding party. The dyke may

however, just be an expensive but elaborate and effective border marker.

Anything that people during the Dark Ages did not understand they would quickly attribute to the devil or some other supernatural being. There are local legends describing how the devil made the dyke. The most popular tells how the devil came uninvited to a wedding party and was chased away by an angry mob. As he ran his tail dragged along the ground, scoring the dyke into the ground and churning the earth up into the embankment.

Reach Lode was dug by the Romans to facilitate the development of Reach as an inland port. A wide range of goods were brought in to trade for the building material, clunch, such as timber and agricultural produce. Commercial traffic dried up with the arrival of the railways in later Victorian times and finished completely in the 1930s. The Lode remains navigable and is used increasingly by narrowboats and other leisure boats. Clunch is a limestone rock; soft when first dug up and very chalky, it becomes harder as it dries out. The stone is often used in buildings in a chequerboard pattern with flint to increase its strength. A quarry close to Reach yielded large quantities of clunch, until supplies ran low; the site has now been replanted as a community wood.

Reach Fair, which is held these days on the May Day Bank Holiday, has always been a grand occasion and still retains its popularity. It was first held in 1201 after receiving a charter from King John, making it one of England's oldest fairs. Custom dictates that it is opened by the Mayor of Cambridge in his robes and chain of office and attended by all the Aldermen in their full ceremonial dress uniform. Part of the opening ceremony has them throwing newly minted penny coins to the crowd. As the fair became more popular there was not enough room and the northern section of Devil's Dyke was levelled to create the present village green.

THE BASICS

Distance: 3¼ miles / 5.2km

Gradient: Mainly flat, two short but steep slopes up embankments

Severity: Easy

Approx. time to walk: 1½ hrs

Stiles: No stiles, gates only

Maps: OS Landranger 154 (Cambridge & Newmarket); Explorer 226 (Ely & Newmarket)

Path description: Hard surfaced paths and grassy paths

Start point: Fair Green in the centre of Reach. (GR TL 568661)

Parking: The car park at Fair Green, Reach at the end of Devil's Dyke; there are some bus services to Reach but check timetables (CB25 0JD)

Dog friendly: Yes

Public toilets: None

Nearest food: The Dyke's End pub at the start/finish

1. Walk out of the car park and on to the Green; this is the site each year of Reach Fair. Continue down to the junction at the bottom left of The Green, and continue straight on down The Hythe to the footbridge on the left and go across.

2. Turn left along this wide track and continue as the surface changes to grass, left and right around Spring Hall to the road. Turn left over the bridge to the signpost.

3. Take the wide byway, Barston Drove to the right, signposted Earthworks Way, and follow this wide track all the way to the road. Turn left for 120 yards to the signpost on the right.

4. Go down the narrow path right/ahead, between trees, bearing right along a left-hand field edge with a hedge to the left and follow the steps down into the disused railway cutting. This dismantled railway used to run between Cambridge and a junction on  the Newmarket to Ely line near Fordham. Turn right to the next set of steps and go up the other side of the cutting. Keep on this path through the dip and up to the top of the Devil's Dyke embankment.

5. Turn left along the path on top of Devil's Dyke, through two gates and down to the village green in Reach village. Turn right, back to the car park on the corner.

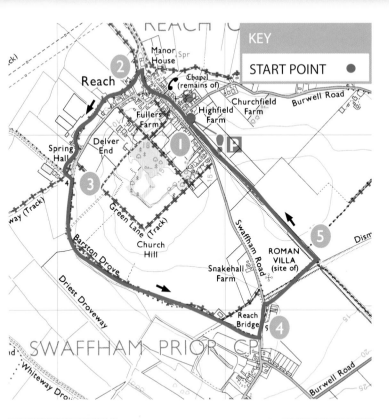

KEY

START POINT ●

GREAT GRANSDEN

Stroll along a quiet green lane away from a sleepy village with a historic windmill.

The impressive lychgate at St Bartholomew's Church was built as a memorial to the men of the village who died in the First World War. The church itself dates from the 15th century, but like a lot of English churches it has suffered from Victorian 'improvement'. The clock mechanism is thought to be late 17th century.

The post mill at Great Gransden is believed to be the oldest in England, dating back to about 1612. The mill worked until 1890 and was given to Cambridgeshire County Council in 1950. The sails, millstones and all the internal machinery are still in place but it was subject to extensive renovation in 1984.

A small stone memorial close to the windmill remembers the World War II airfield at Gransden Lodge, operational from 1942 to 1946. Spitfires, Mustangs, Mosquitos and several heavy bombers including Lancasters were based there. The airfield is now used by Cambridge Gliding Centre.

THE BASICS

Distance: 4 miles / 6.5km

Gradient: Several easy slopes

Severity: Easy

Approx. time to walk: 2 hrs

Stiles: One (not dog friendly)

Maps: OS Landranger 153 (Bedford and Huntingdon); Explorer 208 (Bedford and St Neots)

Path description: Grassy field edges, hard paths and wider hardcore farm roads

Start point: St Bartholomew's Church, Church Road, Great Gransden. (GR TL 271556)

Parking: Small area near the church; limited bus service (check details) (SG19 3AF)

Dog friendly: One stile but not adapted for dogs

Public toilets: None

Nearest food: The Crown and Cushion pub in the village; check opening hours; food at weekends or by arrangement

1. Walk away from the church towards the signposts in the middle of the mini-roundabout; turn left just before, at the signpost, down the wide driveway between the fence and the white house. Go through the narrow metal gate at the next signpost and continue down the hedged/fenced path. Bear left up the slight slope to Main Road.

2. Cross and keep straight on up Dick and Doll's Lane, the bridleway almost opposite. Continue along the right-hand field edge with the trees to the right, into the far right corner, and go through the hedge gap. Bear right on the field edge (trees still right) and then left into the trees at the gap. Take the narrower path left, down the edge of the trees. Keep straight on between the dyke and the field; turn left and right, back to the original direction with the hedge now right, down to the end.

The windsock ahead and some large barnlike buildings mark the location of Little Gransden Airfield, a small grass runway first used in 1966. It is home to a number of small aircraft and related servicing facilities. A very early Hawker Hurricane and an even older Hawker Fury are at present being rebuilt and restored in one of these barns/hangars. Every year the airfield stages a huge airshow and classic car gathering, attracting many thousands of people to this out-of-the-way site, and raising large sums money for charity.

3. Turn right, along this stony/gravelly farm road and the unfenced track which leads past a yellow painted fence post and continues with the hedge to the right, through a gate. Carry on between hedges to the three-way signpost at the barn and turn right. Go through a gate along the track between fences along the avenue of trees.

4. Follow the track right and walk along the path ahead left of the first fence and right of the second fence, up to the corner of Waresley Wood. Turn left and keep direction along the edge of the trees. Waresley Wood is a National Nature Reserve (NNR) and a Site of Special Scientific Interest (SSSI) looked after by the Wildlife Trust for Northamptonshire, Bedfordshire and Cambridgeshire. It contains mainly oak and ash trees. Profuse areas of wildflowers attract a host of butterflies and moths; over five hundred species have been recorded here. The tree cover is home to a great many types of less common birds. The path carries on with a

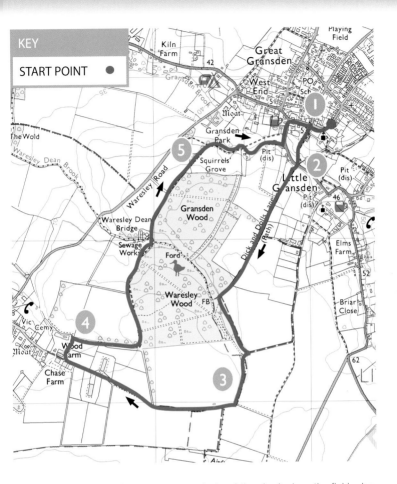

KEY

START POINT ●

wire fence to the left past a sewage plant and then back along the field edge. The church seen to the left above the trees is St James in Waresley village. The original church in Waresley was destroyed by a storm in 1724. The church was later rebuilt but a decision was made during Victorian days to move the church nearer the village. In a strange twist of fate the spire of this replacement church was blown down by the 1987 hurricane and later replaced. Continue to where the edge of the field bears left.

5. Turn right, through the hedge gap and left along the field edge with the trees to the left, bearing right to the stile at the far right. Step over and follow the path and stony driveway ahead to the road at a corner. Turn left into the village, up to the junction and take the road left past the mini-roundabout back to the church.

ELY RIVERSIDE

Ely Cathedral can be seen for miles at the top of its 85-feet (25m) high 'island', once stranded in the middle of marshy fenland. The prominent silhouette of the cathedral with its 200-foot (60m) tower soaring over the surrounding countryside has earned it the nickname 'the Ship of the Fens'.

The settlement dates from the foundation of the abbey by the Saxon princess St Etheldreda in 673. This first abbey was destroyed by the Danes in 870 and not rebuilt for a hundred years. The cathedral itself was not started until 1083. While the cathedral was undergoing reconstruction with the rebuilding of the Lady Chapel in 1322, the central tower collapsed. It was decided not to rebuild the tower and the present octagon was built by Alan of Walsingham, the sacristan or official in charge of the fabric of the cathedral.

The city is built on top of the 'island', which was once surrounded by marshy fenland. The Great Ouse River runs past Ely to the flat landscape where it once just flooded into marshland. Considerable efforts were made to improve the river during the 17th century; 'adventurers', rich men like the Duke of Bedford, put their money into drainage schemes in return for newly reclaimed land. The Dutch engineer Cornelius Vermuyden had the Old and New Bedford Rivers dug between Earith and Denver.

Aldreth Causeway is one of the tracks through the marshes used when Ely was still an island. The route runs north-east from Belsar's Hill, which is believed to be the fort used by the army of William I prior to the 1071 defeat of Hereward. The path, then far less obvious, was revealed by monks after they were bribed by the Normans.

The folk-hero Hereward the Wake based his guerrilla campaign against William the Conqueror on the Isle, then only accessible by boat or a difficult trail through the marshes known only to a few people. He was born sometime in the 1030s in Bourne in Lincolnshire. Little is known of this shadowy figure, with many of the 'facts' of his life coming from fictional sources like Charles Kingsley's Victorian novel and later television series. The rebels sacked Peterborough Abbey and created havoc through the fenland area.

The Danes, however, made a separate peace with King William; the Norman Army was then treacherously shown the way through the marshes to Ely where they defeated Hereward. He is thought to have carried on his resistance for a short while in the desolate fens and then dropped out of history.

Oliver Cromwell lived in the city between 1636 and 1646 in the timber-framed house in St Mary's Street now occupied by the Tourist Information Centre and a museum.

THE BASICS

Distance: 3 miles / 5km

Gradient: Mainly flat, two short but steep slopes

Severity: Easy

Approx. time to walk: 1½ hrs

Stiles: No stiles, gates only

Maps: OS Landranger 154 (Cambridge & Newmarket); Explorer 226 (Ely & Newmarket)

Path description: Tarmac paths, hard surfaced tracks and grassy paths

Start point: The front of the Cathedral, opposite Palace Green. (GR TL 540803)

Parking: Any car park in the city centre (CB7 4DL)

Dog friendly: Yes, but they will need to be on leads on busy streets

Public toilets: Several in the city

Nearest food: Loads of possibilities in the city

1. Facing the cathedral door turn left and immediate right between the grass and the back of the shops; go through the metal gate and turn left through the archway to the High Street. Turn right down to the Market Place and bear left to the far corner.

2. Take the narrow lane past the cul-de-sac sign and follow this road left, down the slight slope between bungalows. Turn right, into Vineyard Way and left at the footpath signpost up the narrow path between fences. Continue over the end of the road and keep straight on with the low wall to the left and the house to the right all the way to the road at the junction with Roswell View.

3. Turn left along the roadside path to the junction at the mini-roundabout and take the road right for 90 yards to the kissing gate on the right. Go through and follow the path through the grass with the trees to the right, to the far end. Cross the footbridge and turn right, along the tarmac road left of Heron House. Roswell pits were created by the extraction of clay called gault, which is a clay used to seal and waterproof the sides of the rerouted rivers and dykes used to drain the fens around Ely. The land around these watercourses dried out and sank, leaving the banks higher than the surrounding countryside, and the gault lining stops them leaking. Most of the former site has been taken over by various forms of wildlife and become a designated Site of Special Scientific Interest (SSSI). The lakes are also used for leisure boating by the Ely Sailing Club. Continue downhill, where the road turns left over a level crossing, to the footpath signpost for the Fen Rivers Way.

4. Bear right, between the hedge and the car park; carry on right, on the hard path with the hedge to the right, parallel to the river. The river has been used for transport since ancient times but never lived up to its potential as too many owners and organisations with vested interests interfered with drainage issues, lock usage and navigation rights; it was well into the 20th century before these problems were resolved. Leisure traffic meanwhile has increased tremendously and there are now substantial fleets of hired and privately owned pleasure craft using the river and marina at Ely. The path passes under the railway bridge and continues to the concrete bridge leading to the marina.

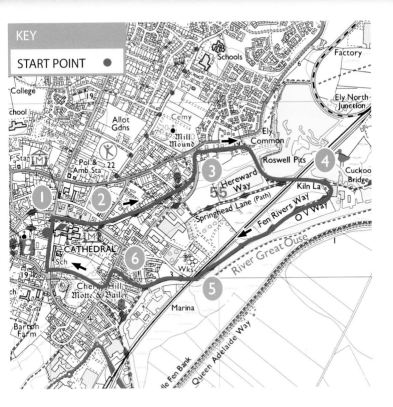

KEY

START POINT ●

5. Go a short distance right to the road and left to the signpost and turn right, through the gap towards the toilets. Continue on the path with the car park to the left, up to the road. Cross and turn left along the roadside path to the impressive castellated gateposts.

6. Turn right, signposted to the Tourist Information Centre. and take the tarmac path uphill through the park. Cherry Hill, the mound off to the left, is the site of Ely Castle. Exit through the archway and turn right, along the roadside path to the front of the cathedral.

LITTLE GIDDING

Little Gidding has twice been the site of religious communities, and was visited twice by the doomed Cavalier King Charles I, but its name is most familiar from the title of one of the poet T.S. Eliot's Four Quartets.

Nicholas Ferrar (1592–1637) was a precocious child born into a well-to-do Elizabethan family. He obtained a degree at Cambridge University and travelled widely in Europe during his twenties. On his return he spent time rescuing the family fortune, which was tied up in the Virginia Company's colony in America, and was briefly Member of Parliament for Lymington. He left London in 1625 and founded the community in the village with the help of his mother, his brother John, his sister Susanna and their families. Their daily life was centred on Christianity and

the Bible, and one person at least was always at prayer. The aim was to combine the best elements of Church of England, Catholic and Puritan practices.

Ferrar died on 4 December 1637; the rigorous life of prayer, recitation of parts of the Bible and religious teaching continued, attracting widespread attention. One of the most important visitors was King Charles I, who came here twice, in 1642 and 1646. Ferrar's brother and sister died within a month of each other in 1647 and the community came to an end, although the family held the estate for some years after.

In 1936 the poet T.S.Eliot visited Little Gidding and was enthralled by the church and its history. The location inspired the last of his Four Quartets although it was not finished until 1942. It proved to be his last piece of poetry, and one of the most popular.

A Friends of Little Gidding society, founded by Alan Maycock, was active from 1946. In 1970 a new community began to use the village as a place of retreat; this became the Society of Christ the Sower and thrived in conjunction with the Friends until it was disbanded in 1998. The Friends were re-established in 2003 and the organisation again flourishes, with its headquarters in Ferrar House on the edge of the village, looking out over the countryside sloping away into the distance.

THE BASICS

Distance: 3 miles / 5km

Gradient: Several easy slopes

Severity: Easy

Approx. time to walk: 1¾ hours

Stiles: One (not dog friendly)

Maps: OS Landranger 142 (Peterborough); Explorer 227 (Peterborough)

Path description: Grassy fields, field edges and wider hardcore farm roads

Start point: Steeple Gidding church, at the end of the village road, 1¾ miles (3km) south-west of the B660 at Great Gidding. (GR TL 132813)

Parking: Small grassy parking area near the church (PE28 5RG)

Dog friendly: One stile but not adapted for dogs

Public toilets: None

Nearest food: Refreshments during the week at Ferrar House in Little Gidding. The Fox and Hounds in Great Gidding (pub only, no food)

LITTLE GIDDING WALK

1. The origins of the Steeple Gidding church go back to the 12th century, but the main building work dates from the 14th century. It was restored during Victorian times. The church has been declared redundant and services are no longer held there; it is now looked after by the Churches Conservation Trust. The building is sometimes used for concerts and meetings. Take the wide broken tarmac track back towards the road. As the track swings left, go through the wide wooden gate on the right. Follow the signposted direction between the two ponds to the stile at the far right.

2. Cross and turn right, down the field edge with the hedge to the right, into the corner and follow the field edge left, with the hedge still right, over the footbridge at the end. Turn right, down to the T-junction of tracks by the power line pole at the bottom.

3. Turn right, along this wide, gravelly farm road and turn left then right. Continue through a boundary with the hedge still on the left; bearing right at the end, through the wide gap with the trees to the right.

4. Turn left into the corner and then right; keep ahead past the end of the substantial footbridge. The waterway to the left is Alconbury Brook, on its way to join the Great Ouse south of Huntingdon. Continue along the field edge with the hedge still left, to the boundary at the far left corner (just past the end of another substantial footbridge). The footbridges are built to take the weight of horses as well as walkers.

5. The route turns right, along the field edge, with the shallow dyke and the trees to the right. At the gate on the right, go through and take a diagonal upslope towards Little Gidding through the first boundary and into the village. The small church used by Ferrar and his family still exists off to the right within its peaceful little graveyard, although it was much restored during the 18th century. The Ferrar Centre, operated by the Friends of Little Gidding, may be open for light refreshments.

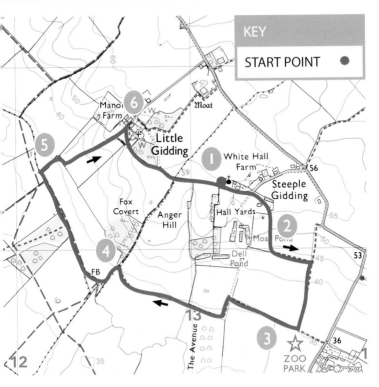

6. Return to the signpost at the edge of the village and bear left across the grass and cross the footbridge to the field edge. Turn left and go through a narrow wooden gate. Continue along the track bearing left to a farm road.

7. Turn right along this brick surfaced road, which soon leads to the parking area close to Steeple Gidding Church.

GRAFHAM WATER

The reservoir near Huntingdon, first known as Diddington Reservoir from the stream going through the valley it was placed in, was planned to alleviate possible water shortages in the East Midlands towns and cities and to supply the projected new town of Milton Keynes.

The main track of tarmac and hardcore goes right around the reservoir, and the walk uses part of this route which is always busy with cyclists, some of whom are travelling quite fast. Please be wary of them, particularly as they approach from the rear.

It was constructed during 1965 and opened by the Duke of Edinburgh in 1966. The reservoir was immediately identified as home by many forms of wildlife, some unusual flora and some reclusive animals that live in the woodland close by. It is, however, the birds that attract most attention; a tremendous variety come and go through the seasons in addition to a large resident population, making it close to heaven for birdwatchers. Over 170 different species of birds have been seen at Grafham.

Grafham Water is the eighth largest reservoir in England and Wales in terms of the volume of water held, with over 57 million cubic metres and the third largest in surface area, has 9 miles (15km) of shoreline.

The deepest point of the reservoir, close to the dam is 60 feet (18m). The surrounding land has a mixture of ancient woodland and more recently planted trees; woodland is fenced only to keep out deer who play havoc with anything they can reach to eat. There is also plenty of grassland and purposely created wetland habitats.

THE BASICS

Distance: 5 miles / 8km

Gradient: Mainly flat, slight slopes only

Severity: Easy

Approx. time to walk: 2½ hrs

Stiles: No stiles, gates only

Maps: OS Landranger 153 (Bedford & Huntingdon); Explorer 225 (Huntingdon & St Ives)

Path description: tarmac paths, hard surfaced tracks and grassy paths

Start point: The parking area at the end of Church Road, just past Hill Farm, heading east out of Grafham village. (GR TL 148693)

Parking: At the start point (PE28 0BE)

Dog friendly: Yes; they will need to be on a lead on the road and in the Grafham Water area

Public toilets: None

Nearest food: The café at the visitor centre on the road south of the village

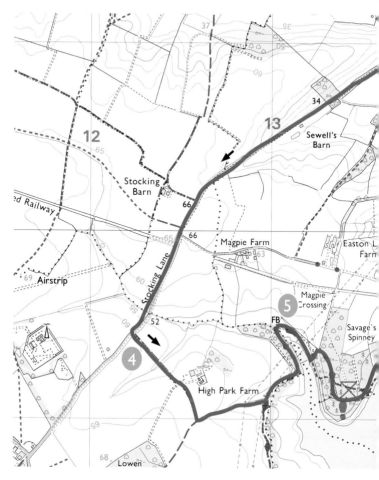

1. Take the wide fenced byway signposted away from the car park, between low fences bearing left parallel to the hardcore Grafham Water circuit track. Bear right, upslope between the hedge on the left and the field. Continue between hedges in a cutting to a disused railway bridge. The railway line once connected Huntingdon and Thrapston.

2. Carry on up the slope; this next section is often very muddy even in dry weather. Bear left and then right downhill and follow the track to a marker post. Bear right the short distance to the narrow road.

3. Take the road left; this is a normal road but does not carry a lot of traffic. Carry on for a mile and a quarter (2km), over the hill and through the dip to the signpost on the left at High Park Farm.

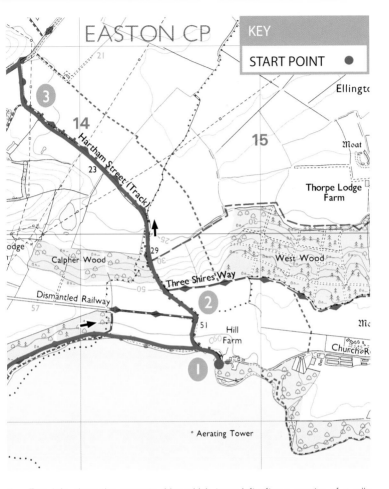

4. Turn left, along the concrete drive which turns left after a quarter of a mile (0.5km); keep straight on along the gravelly farm road. Follow this road left, downslope passing right of the pylons. Bear left with the trees to the right and continue on this Grafham Water circuit track around the inlet, although often not much can be seen when the trees are in leaf and the water at this point is often choked with vegetation.

5. This track leads around some bends and through an area of open ground close to the edge of the reservoir, to the parking area and the start point.

HOUGHTON MILL

July/17

THE PRESENT MILL WAS BUILT IN THE 17TH CENTURY. IT CLOSED IN THE 1930S WHEN IT WAS BOUGHT BY LOCAL PEOPLE AND PRESENTED TO THE NATIONAL TRUST. THE MILL WAS THEN IN USE FOR A LONG TIME AS A YOUTH HOSTEL WHERE, UNUSUALLY FOR THE TIME, SMOKING WAS NOT ALLOWED BECAUSE OF THE FABRIC OF THE BUILDING. THE NATIONAL TRUST HAS NOW PUT THE MILL BACK INTO WORKING ORDER WITH NEW MILLSTONES, MILLING ITS OWN FLOUR AND SELLING IT IN THE SHOP.

The bust in the centre of the village at the end of Mill Lane was erected in 1878 in memory of Potto Brown (1797–1871), a member of the family of Quakers who owned the mill during most of the 19th century. The name Potto was in honour of his grandmother Sarah Potto. Potto Brown's father, William retired in 1821 and the mill and business were run by Potto in partnership with Joseph Goodman. He was always trying out new ideas in the mill, from different blends of flour to looking for the best milling machinery. The successful business expanded into steam technology with mills at St Ives and Godmanchester. He retired in 1862 and spent the rest of his life in charitable and philanthropic activity. Intriguingly he left the Quakers after a local argument in 1837 and became a Congregationalist. He and Goodman founded the chapel in Houghton, and Potto made large donations to other chapels in the area.

The Manor House across the river in Hemingford Abbots was completed in the middle of the 12th century and it is claimed to be the country's oldest continuously inhabited house, a claim that is hotly disputed. The house has achieved fame in literary circles as Green Knowe in the series of books by the author Lucy M. Boston, who lived there from 1939 to her death in 1990. Two other famous residents were the Gunning sisters, born in the house during the 1730s. Maria and Elizabeth were regarded as the most beautiful women in Europe. Maria married the Earl of Coventry, but died aged only 27 from the effects of using fashionable lead-based white make-up. The lead caused eruptions in the skin – which persuaded women to use even more make-up to cover them; Maria contracted blood poisoning and died of the effects. Her sister is famous for marrying two dukes and being the mother of four more. She must have used less make-up as she lived to be 57.

THE BASICS

Distance: 3 miles / 5km

Gradient: Flat

Severity: Easy

Approx. time to walk: 1½ hrs

Stiles: No stiles, gates only

Maps: OS Landranger 153 (Bedford & Huntingdon); Explorer 225 (Huntingdon & St Ives)

Path description: Tarmac paths, hard surfaced tracks and grassy paths

Start point: Houghton Mill, Houghton, Huntingdon. (GR TL 282720)

Parking: Car park at the mill (pay and display, National Trust members free). The village is on a bus route, but check timetables (PE28 2AZ)

Dog friendly: Yes

Public toilets: At the mill

Nearest food: Tearooms in the village and at the mill. The Three Horseshoes pub in the village centre and the Three Jolly Butchers close by in Wyton

HOUGHTON MILL WALK

1. Go past the toilets and bear right along the path through the trees with the river to the right. Carry on through the wooden kissing gate and the trees; the route continues over three substantial footbridges. The massive wooden trestles lurking in the trees are the remains of the railway line that ran between Cambridge and Kettering via St Ives and Huntingdon, which closed in June 1959.

2. Carry on past the sluice; the church with the complete spire is St Margaret's Church in Hemingford Abbots. Further along the church with the truncated spire and flat roof is St James's, Hemingford Grey. This spire collapsed in a storm in 1741 and was never replaced; the remains fell into the river and are still there.

3. At the point where the stream comes in from the left turn sharp left keeping this stream to the right, all the way to the wooden kissing gate. Go through and walk over the substantial, wide concrete bridge with metal handrails. Continue straight on to a staggered crossroads with a tarmac access road.

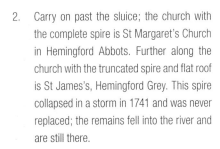

4. Keep straight on, with the wide dyke to the right, across Home Farm Road and the next road and carry on along the now grassy surface, with the dyke still on the right. At St Ives Road, turn left to the village centre where there is a thatched shelter with a clock tower. This is known as the green by local people although there has been no grass growing here for some years. Continue along Mill Road past the church and turn left into the car park.

Be sure to take the first footbridge to the right, NOT the New Footpath ...

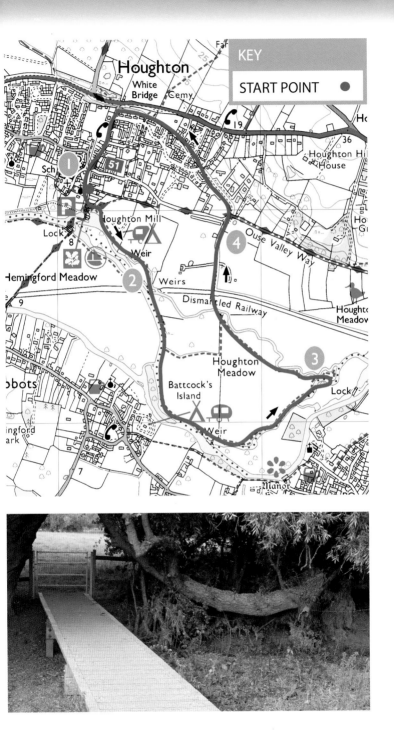

GRANTCHESTER

✓ July / 17

And is there honey still for tea?
The poem about Grantchester and its vicarage was actually written by Rupert Brooke while he was feeling homesick during a trip to Berlin.

The old vicarage in Grantchester was built towards the end of the 17th century and sold by the church in 1820. In 1910 it was the home of Henry Neeve, who rented a room to Rupert Brooke. It is presently owned by a best-selling novelist and his scientist wife.

Rupert Brooke was renowned for his boyish good looks and was described as the handsomest young man in England. At Cambridge he became involved in drama and debate and was briefly a member of the Bloomsbury Group, whose most famous member, Virginia Woolf, boasted of swimming naked with him in Byron's Pool, near Grantchester.

He first lodged in Grantchester in 1909 in Orchard House, which is still open as a tearoom and museum in the village. He moved there to escape a chaotic social life in Cambridge. There was to be no relief, however, as admirers and hangers-on followed him there. The next year he spent some time in Germany, where he wrote 'The Old Vicarage, Grantchester', which does in fact contain a smattering of German words. The poem eulogises Grantchester, but is less than fulsome about other parts of the city, villages close by and their inhabitants. On his return he found that there was no room at Orchard House, his old room having been occupied by someone else, and he had to take a room at the vicarage.

Brooke was born in 1887 in Rugby where his father was a schoolmaster. He won a scholarship to King's College and became a fellow in 1912. He then spent some time travelling, reaching as far as the South Seas and Tahiti where it is said he fathered a child. He was back in this country at the start of the First World War and joined the Royal Naval Volunteer Reserve; he saw action as a sub-lieutenant in the Battle for Antwerp later in the year. He was on board a ship bound for Gallipoli in 1915 when a mosquito bite became infected and he died on 23 April. He was buried on the Greek island of Skyros later that night.

His poetry was becoming popular as he made his final voyage. 'The Soldier' had been read as part of a service in St Paul's Cathedral on 4 April, and his popularity increased as the war continued.

THE BASICS

Distance: 5 miles / 8km or 2½ miles / 4km each way

Gradient: Flat

Severity: Easy

Approx. time to walk: 2½ hrs or up to 1½ hours each way

Stiles: None

Maps: OS Landranger 154 (Cambridge & Newmarket); Explorer 209 (Cambridge)

Path description: Roadside paths and tarmac paths. The track through Paradise Nature Reserve may be muddy.

Start point: Silver Street Bridge in Cambridge. (GR TL 446581)

Parking: Any Cambridge city centre car park (CB3 9ES)

Dog friendly: Yes. Dogs will need to be on a lead in the city streets.

Public toilets: At the west end of the bridge or more in the city centre

Nearest food: Loads of possibilities in the city. The Orchard Tearoom and pubs in Grantchester

GRANTCHESTER WALK

1. Leave the bridge towards the city and turn immediate right down the alleyway Laundress Lane. Cross the cobbled bridge to the right, go through the barrier and turn left along the wide tarmac path with the river to the left. Keep ahead past the sluice and across the canoe rollers. Go under Fen Causeway by the subway.

2. Bear left across the grass to the river, turn right after 80yds, follow the path left and bear right along the track in the grass. Go through the gate and left along the concrete path with the other branch of the river to the left. Cross the bridge to the right.

3 Turn immediate left at the signpost, passing left of the car park, through the kissing gate into Paradise Local Nature Reserve. Follow the path through the trees with the river to the left and exit at the wooden kissing gate on to the road. Turn left and right to the signpost, and take the road Grantchester Meadows between the houses to the left.

4. Continue, passing right of Skaters' Meadow with the solitary headless lampposts in the centre. Skaters' Meadow was used between 1920 and 1940, skaters circling around the old lampposts. Follow the tarmac path with the hedge right and the grass left, running down to the river.

5. At a metal kissing gate and narrow cattle grid close to Grantchester village, the hedge on the right ends and a large field opens out with houses further away at the far edge. Bear right – there is normally a track worn into the grass – to a kissing gate close to a signpost. Go through and turn left along the roadside path to Grantchester village centre where there are several hostelries, a tearoom and a church whose clock will probably not be reading ten to three. Walkers can make a choice here; there is a good bus service back to the centre of Cambridge, or you can walk back. The route is mainly parallel to the outward route, with a couple of alternatives at either end.

6. Take the roadside path towards Trumpington to the path on the left opposite the east end of the church (signposted to Newnham). Turn left, along this path, between fences through the kissing gate; bear right, down to the river and turn left along the path and footbridges closest to the river.

7. Return all the way along the path to the small parking area close to Skaters' Meadows on the outskirts of Newnham. Carry on between houses to the fork in

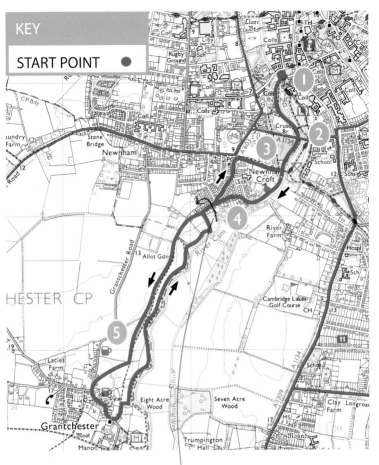

the road and bear left along Eltisley Avenue to the junction, then turn left along Grantchester Street to the traffic lights.

8. Take the narrow access road to the right or walk parallel to the road along the edge of Lammas Land (the café/snack bar may be open) and keep this direction along the track to the right and cross the footbridge. Bear left on the concrete path at the further branch of the river. With the river to the right, walk up nearly to Fen Causeway and bear left under the subway.

9. Continue on the path with the river still right, over the canoe rollers and past the sluice. At the end turn right, through the barriers and left along Laundress Lane to Silver Street.

PARK IN GRANTCHESTER TO CUT OUT BORING SUBURBAN SECTION

LADY GROVE

THE WALK MAKES USE OF PATHS IN WOODLAND AND
FARMLAND FURTHER AWAY FROM THE EDGE OF THE
RESERVOIR AT GRAFHAM WATER. THE LAST THIRD OF THE
WALK IS ON PART OF THE TRACK WHICH CIRCUMNAVIGATES
THE RESERVOIR, WHICH IS USUALLY VERY BUSY WITH
CYCLISTS, SO DO BE AWARE OF THEM AND THEIR MUCH
GREATER SPEED.

The reservoir has become one of the premier leisure destinations in Cambridgeshire since it was opened by the Duke of Edinburgh in 1966. There are excellent facilities to walk, cycle, sail, windsurf, fish or sit down and enjoy the view with a cup of tea. The reservoir was created by damming the valley of Diddington Brook, with water pumped mainly from the River Ouse at Offord.

Grafham Water Nature Reserve, at the western end of the reservoir, was designated a Site of Special Scientific Interest (SSSI) in 1986. The reserve is looked after by the Wildlife Trust for Bedfordshire, Cambridgeshire and Northamptonshire. The woodland is regularly thinned out by the removal of large trees to let light into the lower levels, encouraging growth of wildflowers and ground cover plants. Woodcock and other more unusual woodland birds use the reserve. No fishing is allowed at this end of the reservoir, creating a bird sanctuary that is already showing positive results with the visits of the rare Slavonian grebe, the spectacular osprey and the avocet, the iconic symbol of successful wildlife renewal.

Littless Wood is one of the oldest tracts of woodland in the area, first planted during the 1600s; the hide within the wood gives views across the bird sanctuary to the shallower water at the edge. The reservoir here feeds dabbling ducks, sifting through the water for plant material to eat. Further out, diving ducks, cormorant and grebe hunt for fish.

Gaynes Hall, set in parkland south of Perry village, is a recently restored Georgian Mansion. It had been owned by the Duberley family from 1797 until its requisition by the government in 1940.

It became Station 61 of the Special Operations Executive. Wartime agents were kept here until weather and other conditions were right for them to be parachuted or landed in Occupied Europe. Between 1945 and 1983 the hall was used as an administration block for Gaynes Hall Borstal. After the closure and demolition of the secure accommodation, Littlehey Prison was built on the site. The Hall has been used for offices; it is now a food and lifestyle school.

Historically the village of Perry was separated by open land: East Perry was part of Great Staughton parish and West or Gaynes Perry was part of the parish of Grafham. The reservoir separated West Perry from Grafham and new housing had filled the gaps between East and West Perry. The two ends were consequently combined into a new parish in the mid-1960s.

THE BASICS

Distance: 3¾ miles / 6km

Gradient: Mainly flat, slight slopes only

Severity: Easy

Approx. time to walk: 1¾ hrs

Stiles: No stiles, gates only

Maps: OS Landranger 153 (Bedford & Huntingdon); Explorer 225 (Huntingdon & St Ives)

Path description: Tarmac paths, hard surfaced tracks and grassy paths which may be muddy in the wet

Start point: Mander car park off the B661 at the western end of Perry village. (GR TL 144671)

Parking: At the start (pay and display). Limited bus service (PE28 0BX)

Dog friendly: Yes; they will need to be on a lead in the Grafham Water area

Public toilets: At the café

Nearest food: The café on site and the Wheatsheaf pub in Perry village

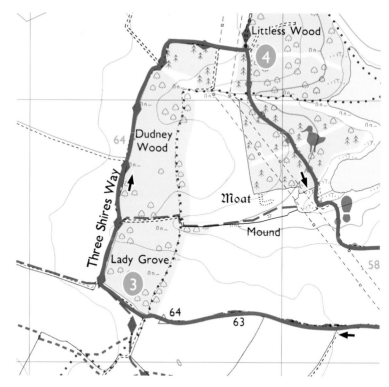

1. Go out of the narrow gate at the far end of the car park; carry on through the grassy area on the hardcore path, through the trees to the main tarmac-surfaced Grafham Water circuit track, close to a bird hide. Keep on this track to where it swings right, close to a pylon.

2. Keep straight on, along the farm track on the right-hand field edge, with the dyke to the right to a gap close to the first boundary. Go through the gap and turn left, back to the original direction with the hedge now left. Continue to the corner. Bear left, through the gap and right, on the field edge with the trees of Lady Grove to the right, to the marker post at the corner.

3. Turn right, to where a more substantial access road comes out of the trees, and

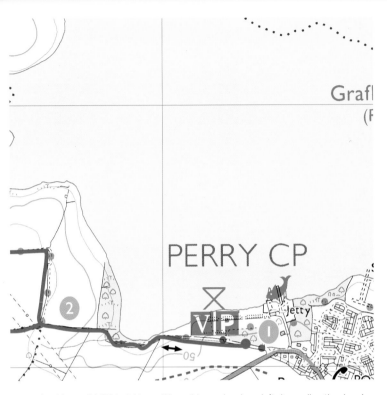

take this road left/straight on. When this road swings left, keep direction bearing right, to a marker post. Take the track left/straight on, between hedge and trees

up to the corner; follow the track right to a clearing where the power lines go through and carry on to the end. Bear left, to the Grafham Water circuit track and turn right to the information board. There are a series of nature walks here through Littless Wood that are an option at this point.

4. Keep on this main path which leads round several corners to the pylon at point 2 passed earlier. Continue along this path back to the car park and the starting point. Do allow for the fact that the main path goes to the right of the car park.

MARE WAY

Mare Way is an ancient ridgeway running east from the A1198 along a minor road; it continues along a grassy bridleway, bearing south, towards the A603 but doesn't quite make it all the way.

Several radio telescope dishes may be seen from the higher vantage point as Mare Way goes along the hill. These are part of the Mullard Radio Astronomy Observatory at Lord's Bridge. The location was a railway station situated in open countryside on the 'Varsity Line' between Cambridge and Oxford. In the Second World War the site was converted to a massive ammunition store. After the closure of the line in 1967 the observatory took over the site and built a wide range of radio telescopes. The Ryle telescope consisted of eight antennae, four of which were fixed; the other four were mounted on trolleys which could move up and down the old railway line on a specially built 20-foot-gauge railway.

Sir Martin Ryle (1918–84) had worked on radar during World War II. After the war he was behind the development of radio astronomy in Cambridge in the early 1950s and became its first professor. He was the founding director of the Mullard Radio Astronomy Observatory in 1957. He went on to share the 1974 Nobel Prize for Physics with Anthony Hewish for their work in astronomical research; he was Astronomer Royal from 1972 to 1982.

THE BASICS

Distance: 4 miles / 6.5km

Gradient: Mainly flat, one slope up and then back down near to the finish

Severity: Easy to moderate

Approx. time to walk: 2 hrs

Stiles: None, gates only

Maps: OS Landranger 154 (Cambridge & Newmarket); Explorer 209 (Cambridge)

Path description: Roads, wide farm tracks, hard surfaced and grassy paths which may be muddy in the wet

Start point: St Helens Church, Church Lane, Little Eversden. (GR TL 375533)

Parking: Considerate roadside parking in the village (CB23 1HQ). There is also a bus service, check timetables

Dog friendly: Yes

Public toilets: None

Nearest food: The Hoops Tandoori Restaurant, High Street, Great Eversden

MARE WAY WALK

1. Go back along Church Lane to the junction and turn left on the High Street, past the black barn, to the signpost on the right. Go through the metal kissing gate. Walk along the tarmac path between the hedge and the fence, through the next kissing gate and keep straight on, with the hedge now right, and go through the wooden gate at the end. Continue up the narrow lane and through the gate at the end.

2. Bear left across the narrow road, through the kissing gate and go down the path between the hedge and the single-rail concrete and pipe fence. Bear slight left at the end through a metal kissing gate and a narrow wooden gate. Keep straight on to the opposite corner of this field, through the gate and on to the road.

3. Turn right, past the church and take the wide grassy path to the left passing right of the church and continue slight right between hedges down to the end. Take the track right, between houses to the road.

4. Turn left and carry on along the farm road between the buildings at Merrys Farm. Keep ahead slight left and right, upslope between trees, all the way to the crossroads of wide tracks at the concrete reservoirs.

5. The route goes to the left along wide Mare Way, between trees; continue for nearly a mile (1.5km) to the marker post at the end.

6. Turn left, along this wide grassy path between hedges down to the bottom and bear right to a wide track on the left. Turn left, over the rise passing right of the farm buildings, all the way to the road. Keep ahead up High Street to the starting point.

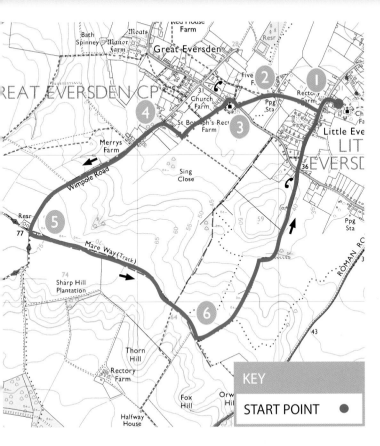

MOW FEN

The walk crosses the controversial Cambridgeshire Guided Busway. The route is mainly along embankments and quiet country byways in the river meadows north of Cambridge. One of the water meadows can get very wet after heavy rain. The walker will be unlucky not to see kingfishers, grey herons and little egrets in this marshy landscape.

The route of the new busway between Cambridge and Huntingdon runs along the course of the disused railway line connecting the two locations. The last passenger train ran along this track in 1970, but the line from St Ives to Cambridge was in use until 1993 transporting sand, gravel and aggregates from the pits at Fen Drayton to various destinations still on the rail system. The line first opened in 1847 and had been recommended for closure in the 1963 Beeching Report.

The ongoing congestion on the almost parallel A14 persuaded Cambridgeshire County Council to develop the disused line as a guided busway. A fair-sized and influential group was behind a plan to convert the line into a modern tramway system but controversy followed the planning and construction of the busway, forcing the whole thing into a public inquiry. The Council finally approved the plans in 2005.

Construction commenced in March 2007 with the opening of a factory in Longstanton manufacturing the sleepers and beams for the track, a highly technical operation making the items to a one-millimetre tolerance. Tests were conducted on the completed sections during 2008, but a January 2009 announcement put the opening back until the summer. Further delays were declared in the summer and autumn.

A major disagreement between the council and the busway contractors delayed the opening until August 2011, triggering legal proceedings involving the two parties which were only completed by an out-of-court settlement in August 2013.

Emerging from the chaos of its inception, the busway is proving very popular, with two-and-a-half-million journeys during the first year. It does mean that the regular sound of a passing bus is added to the distant but muted buzz of the traffic on the A14. Don't be fooled by the thought that the busway is a showcase of transport technology; the bus is not driven by a robot or completely on automatic. There is still a competent driver on board to operate the vehicle. The advantages are that he does not have to steer on the busway and there is no other traffic; notice the car traps near crossings to prevent joyriding. When the bus reaches ordinary roads in Cambridge, the driver takes full control of the vehicle, to its destination anywhere in the city.

Nearby Fen Drayton Lakes in the disused gravel workings is now an RSPB reserve. The location was already a popular location for common British birds, and more exotic birds are now beginning to find this excellent setting. Recent sightings include bittern, smew and the great white egret (they are much, much bigger than the little egret). Sand lizards can often be seen basking in the sunshine, and dragonflies and damselflies are abundant at the right time. Otters are normally present in the reserve but some patience may be required, hanging around until they believe you have gone.

THE BASICS

Distance: 4¼ miles / 7km

Gradient: Mainly flat, slight slopes up or down embankments only

Severity: Easy

Approx. time to walk: 2¼ hrs

Stiles: Three

Maps: OS Landranger 153 (Bedford & Huntingdon); Explorer 225 (Huntingdon & St Ives)

Path description: Tarmac paths, hard surfaced tracks and grassy paths

Start point: The small parking area at the end of Chain Road, a mile from the start of the road in Over village. (GR TL 363713)

Parking: Small car park just over the hump in the road. Bus services to Over (start walk from the village) (CB24 5NT)

Dog friendly: No

Public toilets: None

Nearest food: The Admiral Vernon and the Exhibition in Over village

MOW FEN WALK

1. Go through the kissing gate on top of the embankment, signposted to Over along the path on top of the embankment to the point where it starts to bear left. Bear right, across the footbridge at Webb's Hole Sluice. Bear left with the path, still on top of an embankment to a point above a footbridge.

2. Descend the path and cross the footbridge with the stiles at both ends. Bear right, across what can be a very wet field, over the stiles at the boundaries and through the kissing gate at the end. Go up the steps to the wide farm road between hedges.

3. Turn right along this road to the busway; cross carefully, as the buses travel quite fast here, and follow the wide track left to the road in Swavesey.

4. Take the road right, past the pond and turn right, up Taylor's Lane, bearing right, past the 'Pedestrians' warning signpost and the cemetery, to the signpost. Keep straight on, signposted Mow Fen, and cross back over the busway.

5. Continue along this road to Mow Fen Lake and follow it left to the top of the embankment. Turn right, between the wide dyke and the lake to the footbridge on the left. Cross and turn right, back to the original direction with the dyke now on the right, up to the T-junction of tracks.

6. Turn right, over the footbridge on top of the sluice. Keep on this path on top of the embankment with the River Great Ouse to the left, all the way back to Webb's Hole Sluice and join the outward route back to the parking area.

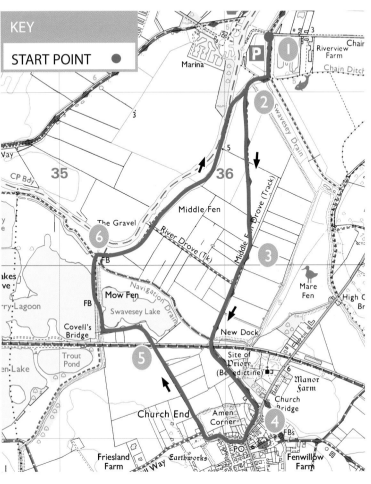

KEY

START POINT ●

Marina

Riverview Farm

Chain Ditch

Swavesey Drain

Way

CP Bdy

35

36

Middle Fen

The Gravel

River Drove (Tk)

Middle Fen Drove (Track)

FB

Mare Fen

High

akes ve

Navigation Drain

Mow Fen

FB

Swavesey Lake

Trout Pond

ry Lagoon

Covell's Bridge

New Dock

Site of Priory (Benedictine)

Manor Farm

Church Bridge

en Lake

Church End

Amen Corner

PO

FBs

Friesland Farm

Earthworks

Way

Fenwillow Farm

OLD WEST RIVER

Stretham Old Engine is a potent symbol of our ancestors' constant fight to keep the reclaimed farmland free from flooding. It is also a sobering thought how difficult it must have been to get the heavy and unwieldy pieces of the engine into place in such a remote location.

When the fens were first drained in the 17th century the surrounding farmland was about the same level as the dykes that had been dug to take the water away. Small wind-powered pumps were quite adequate to lift the collected water from the land into these drains. As the years passed and the once waterlogged fens dried out the land sank lower and lower, making the operation far more difficult.

The problem was not finally solved until the advent of steam power in the early 19th century. Nearly a hundred massive beam engines operated by steam were built, driving large wooden wheels capable of scooping water from the low-lying fens into the higher drains. Stretham Old Engine was built by Butterleys in Derbyshire and installed in 1831, with a beam nearly 25 feet (8m) in width. It drove a 37-foot (11m) scoop wheel capable of lifting 150 tons of water per minute into the adjacent river. The engine replaced several local drainage mills and worked for over a century until a modern diesel engine driving a centrifugal pump took over in 1925.

The steam engine remained on standby for a number of years but was last used during the floods of 1940; it last ran under its own power a year later. In the 21st century it is preserved in running condition but powered by an electric motor for demonstration purposes only. A series of smaller, more versatile, electrically operated pumps situated nearby on the River Cam now do the same job much more efficiently. The redundant diesel engine has also been preserved and can be seen on site. The three boilers used had to raise a considerable amount of steam and ate up a ton of coal every four hours; the coal, however, was easily transported to the engine by a barge unloading right outside.

THE BASICS

Distance: 5½ miles / 9km

Gradient: Mainly flat, several easy slopes

Severity: Easy

Approx. time to walk: 2½ hrs

Stiles: None

Maps: OS Landranger 154 (Cambridge & Newmarket); Explorer 226 (Ely & Newmarket)

Path description: Grassy field edges and embankments, hard paths and wider hardcore farm roads

Start point: St James's Church, High Street, Stretham. (GR TL 512746)

Parking: Considerate roadside parking in the village (CB6 3LD)

Dog friendly: Dogs will need to be on leads near cattle

Public toilets: None

Nearest food: There is a Chinese takeaway on Newmarket Road. The Red Lion pub near the church and a shop/post office close by

OLD WEST RIVER WALK

1. Go back to the main A1123, cross with care and keep ahead up Cage Lane. Continue straight on between the wall and the hedge to the road, turn left and walk up to the end. Carry on along the short length of track with the hedge to the left. At the footbridge turn right and take the path with the dyke left, between hedges; cross the footbridge and keep ahead on the field edge with the dyke still left, all the way down to the kissing gate and footbridge at the wider track.

2. Turn left, along this track with the dyke now left, bearing right, then left to the narrow road. Turn right and walk across the bridge over the Old West River, which is what this section of the River Great Ouse is called.

3. Take the path to the left, with the river to the left, past Stretham Old Engine, and bear left to the path on top of the embankment. Continue to the A1123. Cross carefully and continue on the path bearing right, around the right-hand corner and under the railway, to the footbridge at Popes Corner. This is the confluence where the River Cam joins the River Great Ouse, although the Cam looks the bigger river at this point. There used to be a pub here called the Fish and Duck, the name now taken by the marina on the site.

4. Cross the river and turn left, back under the railway and bear right, up the wide path with the trees to the left. Keep on the track bearing right, to the marker post and turn left, between fields to the stony farm road.

5. Turn left and follow the road right and left, between buildings at the farmyard of Plantation Farm and carry on up the concrete road into Stretham. Turn right and follow the road left to the T-junction, turn right, up to the next junction and take Top Street to the left. The picturesque windmill at the north end of Stretham is now a privately owned house. At the end, turn left down to the church.

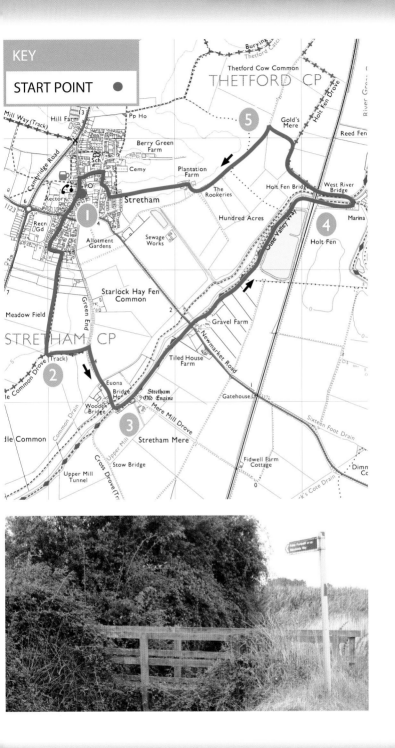

RIVER MEL

The church tower at Meldreth looks as if it is still waiting for someone to come along and finish it. The village is very proud of its position on the Greenwich Meridian and erected a marker stone in 1999.

The River Mel is unusually a chalk stream. Water from rainfall collects in natural underground reservoirs or aquifers below the chalk uplands on the Cambridgeshire border with Essex and Hertfordshire. The chalk filters the water and it is very pure when it enters the river at its source, the springs around Melbourn Bury. It remains very clear, above a stony gravelly bed, one of the reasons why chalk streams are so good for fish and wildlife further up the food chain like kingfishers, water voles and otters. The river continues from its source, flowing past the edges of Melbourn and Meldreth and north to join the arm of the River Cam known as the Rhee.

Meldreth was at the centre of a fertiliser boom during the 19th century. Coprolites are the organic remains of dinosaurs and marine organisms deposited here in the Cretaceous and Jurassic periods. It was found to be rich in phosphates and easy to mine in this area as it was found very close to the surface. Rising costs, deeper and more difficult mining conditions, coupled with cheaper imports such as South American guano (bird droppings, again rich in phosphates) and artificial fertiliser finished the business by the end of the century.

A set of stocks and a whipping post survive near the village sign on Marvell's Green, where the high street joins North End and Fenny Lane. Records report the last use of the stocks was in 1860.

Meldreth has a station on the busy Cambridge to King's Cross railway line, making the village an attractive residential option for anyone wishing to commute to London or Cambridge.

THE BASICS

Distance: 3 miles / 5km

Gradient: Flat

Severity: Easy

Approx. time to walk: 1½ hrs

Stiles: 2 easy, 2 harder

Maps: OS Landranger 154 (Cambridge & Newmarket); Explorer 209 (Cambridge)

Path description: Grassy fields and field edges, hard paths and wider hardcore farm roads

Start point: Holy Trinity Church, North End, Meldreth. (GR TL 377468)

Parking: Small parking area opposite the church (SG8 6NR)

Dog friendly: No, two difficult stiles

Public toilets: None

Nearest food: The British Queen pub and a shop/post office in the High Street

RIVER MEL WALK

1. Facing the church turn right, along the roadside path over the easily missed bridge across the River Mel to the signpost at the corner. Turn right, past the information board, bearing right with the ditch and the trees to the right. Carry on along this stony road to the railway and cross this busy line with care.

2. Continue along the wide track between fields, across the stile to the A10, cross this deceptively busy road carefully and go over the stile on the other side. Keep straight on over this field, which may be under cultivation although a path should be well marked. Cross the footbridge and the next field, which again might have a crop in, to the farm road.

3. Turn right, along this grass then tarmac track passing right of the allotments, to the signpost at the corner close to the A10. Take the road left into the outskirts of Melbourn to the signpost on the right.

4. The route goes to the right along the concrete driveway between wooden and metal fences, passing right of the nursery and up the edge of the sports field to the left of the strikingly painted pavilion, back to the river in the far right corner.

5. Turn right, along the well-made path with the River Mel to the left, back under the A10. Carry on along the left-hand field edge to the boundary; bear left then right to the railway where there is a choice. A restricted height path goes under the bridge for dogs and children or there are stiles and a crossing place for those who do not want to bend.

6. Keep ahead now with the river still left, bearing right along the left-hand field edge to the kissing gate near Topcliffe Watermill. The mill was the property of St Thomas's Hospital in London between 1553 and 1948. Go through and follow the path and driveway to the road near the church and parking area.

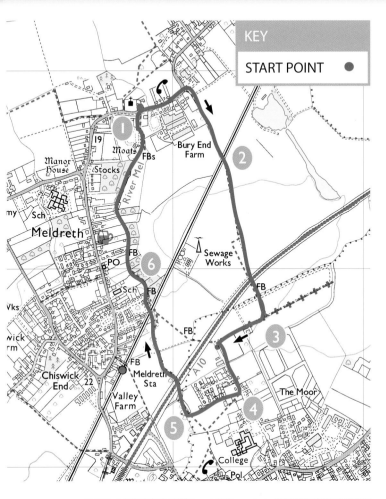

KEY

START POINT ●

WANDLEBURY RING

An Iron Age fort nestling in trees and the tale of an unknown but important horse resting peacefully under a busy country park.

The first ring of the Iron Age hill fort at Wandlebury was dug in around 400 BCE; a ditch and ramparts were augmented by a wooden palisade. A footpath runs around the base of the ditch. A second ring was dug inside the first in the first century BCE. There is some archaeological evidence of Roman occupation during the first years after the invasion.

The stable block is the surviving part of a large house built here in 1685 for King James II; it later passed into the ownership of the Earl of Godolphin, who ran a stud farm at Babraham near Cambridge. The house itself was demolished in 1956. The site is now looked after by the organisation Cambridge Past, Present & Future.

The horse known as the Godolphin Barb was foaled in Arabia in 1724 and traded several times, eventually being given as a present to the French monarch Louis XV in 1730. It was rumoured to have been used to pull carts around Paris. Bought by the English aristocrat Edward Coke, it was later sold to the Earl of Godolphin. Initially the horse was used as a 'teaser' to arouse the interest of horses ready for covering, but the horses that were sired by the Barb were extremely fast and he became champion sire for three years during the middle of the 18th century.

Godolphin Barb, also known as the Godolphin Arabian, is one of the three stallions from which all modern racehorses are descended. He died at Wandlebury on Christmas Day 1753 and was buried under the archway of the stable block.

THE BASICS

Distance: 3 miles / 5km

Gradient: Several easy slopes

Severity: Easy

Approx. time to walk: 1½ hrs

Stiles: None

Maps: OS Landranger 154 (Cambridge & Newmarket); Explorer 209 (Cambridge)

Path description: All good hard surfaces, one short roadside path next to the busy A1307

Start point: The car park at Wandlebury Country Park, off the A1307 south-east of Cambridge (GR TL 492533)

Parking: Pay and display car park. Bus services pass on the A1307 (CB22 3AE)

Dog friendly: Yes

Public toilets: At the visitor centre

Nearest food: Refreshments at the visitor centre

WANDLEBURY RING WALK

1. Take the footpath from the car park signposted to Wormwood Hill, through the trees with the A1307 to the right, and keep direction across the lower slope of the tumuli to the roadside path. Turn left to the byway signpost.

2. Turn left along this wide stony track, upslope and then bearing right down to the T-junction of tracks. This peaceful looking track was once a busy Roman road running between Colchester and Chester, passing through Leicester on the way. The road was built primarily to facilitate the rapid movement of troops in the turbulent years following the Roman invasion. There would also have been considerable commercial traffic during the peaceful years after the conquest and the long period of 'Pax Romana' until their departure in the early years of the 5th century. The road fell into disuse and dilapidation during the Dark

Ages. When people started to travel more widely during later centuries they often used far different routes, although the track of the present A14 between Cambridge and Godmanchester is believed to follow the Roman road. The road was unnamed by the Romans, but 18th-century archaeologists and antiquarians coined the 'Via Devana' name derived from the Chester or 'Deva' road.

3. Take this track left past the information board for 20 yards and go through the wooden kissing gate on the left. Follow the wide track ahead through the trees to the signpost at the junction; take the track right and follow left to the wide wooden gate. Turn right and keep ahead, right/straight on, still through trees to a signpost and turn right, to the Ely viewpoint.

4. Go back and carry on in the same direction along the path just left, past the open ground. Turn right, between the trees and fence and carry on, veering left. This is Telegraph Clump, at 246 feet (75m) one of the highest points in Cambridgeshire. The hill was the site during the first half of the 19th century of a telegraph station, one of a series between London and Yarmouth sending messages by semaphore on mechanically operated shutters. The system soon became redundant with the invention of the much

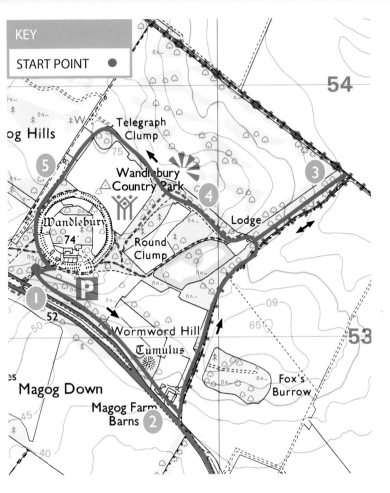

KEY

START POINT ●

54

og Hills

Telegraph Clump

5

Wandlebury Country Park

3

4

Wandlebury

74

Round Clump

Lodge

52

50

P

1

Wormword Hill

09

65

53

Magog Down

Cumulus

45

Magog Farm Barns

2

Fox's Burrow

40

more sophisticated and reliable electric telegraph using Morse Code. Go around a loop and down the path between hedge and trees leading to the raised rings of the Iron Age fort.

5. Turn right and continue along the path with the ring to the left, bearing right to the car park and the starting point.

WICKEN FEN

WICKEN FEN IS ONE OF THE NATIONAL TRUST'S OLDEST PROPERTIES; IT HAS BEEN IN THEIR CARE SINCE ITS PURCHASE IN 1899. THE FIRST AREA WAS ONLY TWO ACRES, FOR WHICH THEY PAID £10. THE FEN IS BOTH A NATIONAL NATURE RESERVE AND A SITE OF SPECIAL SCIENTIFIC INTEREST (SSSI); IT IS ONE OF ONLY FOUR FENS THAT SURVIVE IN THEIR ORIGINAL CONDITION.

The National Trust land now includes fen, farmland, reedbeds and marshland. There is a rich variety in all forms of flora and fauna and an enormous range of plants and invertebrates living in the reserve. The list of bird visitors particularly is extensive, containing vast numbers of more frequently seen birds coexisting with less common species.

The iconic wooden windmill situated on the fen was originally located on the edge of Adventurers' Fen. It was moved to its present position in the 1950s. A major repair has just been completed after its sails were damaged in a storm at the end of 2013. The mill normally runs on Sunday afternoons during the summer. These days it is used to replenish the water table with clean river water, rather than its original task of draining the land.

The National Trust has a plan, which it hopes to complete over the next 100 years, to increase the size of its holding in the area to 22 square miles (56 sq. km), by purchasing land at its current value as it becomes available.

THE BASICS

Distance: 5 miles / 8km

Gradient: Flat, with some minimal slopes up embankments

Severity: Easy

Approx. time to walk: 2½ hrs

Stiles: No stiles, gates only

Maps: OS Landranger 154 (Cambridge & Newmarket); Explorer 226 (Ely & Newmarket)

Path description: Hard surfaced paths and grassy paths along the tops of the embankments, which may be muddy in the wet

Start point: Wicken Fen National Nature Reserve, Lode Lane, Wicken. (GR TL 563705)

Parking: The National Trust car park on Lode Lane (CB7 5XP) (pay and display, National Trust members free). There are bus services to Wicken but check timetables

Dog friendly: Yes

Public toilets: In the car park

Nearest food: The Maid's Head pub and the National Trust Wicken Fen Cafe

WICKEN FEN WALK

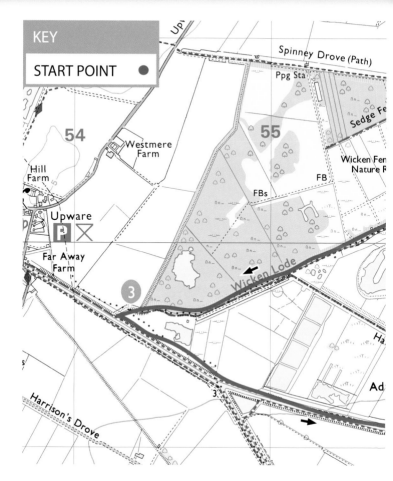

1. Turn left out of the car park entrance, past the toilets and keep straight on. Fen Cottage to the left is a recreation of a typical cottage, lived in by workers in the Wicken Fen area. The wooden wind pump familiar from so many illustrations of the fen can be seen to the right and a little further on is a more modern metal wind pump. Carry on up the stony/gravelly road with Wicken Lode to the right. Turn left with the track to a wide wooden bridge with no handrails.

2. Cross the bridge and turn right, back to the original direction with the lode still right. The thatched lookout post 33feet (10m) high towering above the trees is a bird hide giving a terrific view of bird life at the tree tops. Continue all the way to the footbridge at Burwell Lode.

3. Turning right across the footbridge here and following the footpath, for just over half a

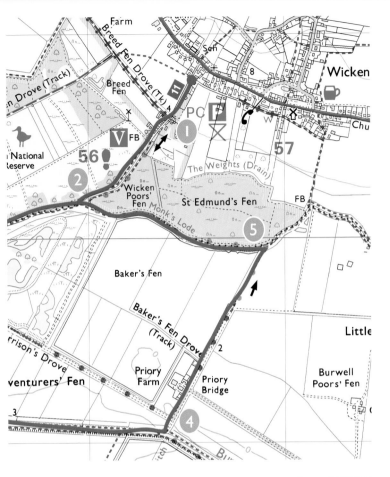

mile (1km) along the bank of Reach Lode, leads to the hamlet of Upware, where there was once a chain ferry across the river. There was a pub here from the 18th century to cater for passing river traffic; originally the Black Swan, it became the Lord Nelson after his death in 1806. The pub later became the Five Miles from anywhere: no Hurry, but was demolished after a fire in the mid-1950s. It opened again in a new building in 1995. We need to turn left, past the stile along the path with Burwell Lode

to the right and carry on, bearing left past the junction with Reach Lode. The land off to the left is Adventurers' Fen, currently grazed by a mixture of Highland cattle and Konik ponies which originate in Poland. Adventurers were the people who provided the money, in an 'adventure', to drain the fens. Keep straight on to the distinctive Cockup Bridge.

4. There are now two bridges here; the original Cockup Bridge was a substantially built hump-backed wooden bridge that could be used by pedestrians and horses. This was replaced in the mid-1990s by the present concrete bridge, which is accessible for pedestrians, difficult for cyclists and impossible for horses. The other bridge is an electrically operated lift bridge, owned and operated by the Environment Agency, capable of taking a small but heavy vehicle on to the access roads for maintenance work on the various Lodes. Take the wide track left, past the car park and Priory Farm. Keep straight on along this stony farm track to marker post 11 at the junction of cycleways.

5. Turn left, along this path with Monk's Lode and St Edmunds fen to the right, to the junction of paths and footbridge at point 2. Turn right and follow the outward route back to the car park.

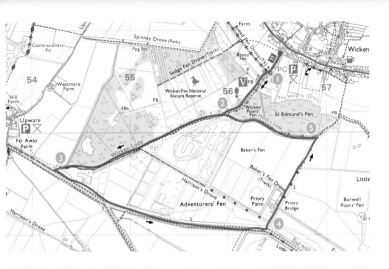

WIMPOLE PARK

Sunday morning visitors to this popular and busy National Trust location may find themselves competing with the weekly 5km run around the parkland.

The park has a folly in the grounds; a semi-ruined castle was commissioned in 1751 by the 1st Earl of Hardwicke and built by Capability Brown in 1769. It is a substantial installation over 200 feet (60m) in length and four stories high.

The house here was completed in 1650; it was built by Thomas Chicheley, whose family had held the property for over 250 years. Debt forced him to sell the house in 1689; it passed through the hands of several aristocratic families to the hands of the 1st Earl of Hardwicke in 1740. Viscount Clifden owned the property in the first part of the 20th century, but when the 6th Viscount died in 1930, his son the 7th Viscount, who lived in Lanhydrock House in Cornwall, leased the Wimpole Estate to George and Elsie Bambridge. Elsie was the only surviving child of the author Rudyard Kipling. After his death in 1936 she bought the property and used his legacy and the continuing royalties from his books to restore Wimpole to its former glories. Elsie died childless in 1976 and left the estate to the National Trust.

THE BASICS

Distance: 5½ miles / 9km

Gradient: Mainly flat, one easy slope up close to the start

Severity: Easy

Approx. time to walk: 2½ hrs

Stiles: One

Maps: OS Landranger 154 (Cambridge & Newmarket); Explorer 209 (Cambridge). One short section of a few yards is on Explorer 208 (Bedford & St Neots).

Path description: Estate roads, grassy parkland, well-used woodland paths which may be muddy and have trip hazards, field edges, hard paths and wider hardcore farm roads

Start point: National Trust car park on the Wimpole Estate, Arrington. (GR TL 336510)

Parking: Large National Trust car park (SG8 0BW) (pay and display; NT members free)

Dog friendly: No, one difficult stile, one difficult gate and cattle grids

Public toilets: On the property

Nearest food: The NT Stable Café and shop close by

✓ August 201

1. Go back to the entrance road and the metal fence, turn right and walk away from the entrance towards the parkland, passing right of the stable building and clock tower. Keep on this narrow tarmac estate road over a cattle grid to the cattle grid at the fence close to the gate at the road. The road passing the gates used to be numbered A14; in the still extant system where main roads leaving to the right of the A1 or Great North Road were numbered in the A10–19 section, Ermine Street was considered important enough to be the first road after London to be in this section even though it headed back towards Royston. In a review of the system in the early 90s, the new A1–M1 link road extending down to Felixstowe was considered more deserving of the number and Ermine Street became the A1198.

START

2. Turn ~~right~~ *left* along the edge of the parkland with the fence and the trees to the left. Walk into the corner and turn right, upslope; bear right with the fence through/past a gate *before lake, bear left* which may be locked. Continue through the kissing gate along the avenue of trees, to the wide wooden gate ~~on the left close to an information board.~~ *and enter woodland*

In woodland,

3. ~~Cross the metal step/stile and~~ take the wide track to the right, ~~between trees~~; carry on around the corners to a substantial junction, at a marker post *just before* ~~close to~~ open land.

through a strip woodland

4. Turn right and keep the same direction. This track leads eventually to a signpost at a junction with a tarmac road. Take the road left to the signpost at the corner where the road swings left.

Follow map!

✓ 5. Turn right, up the first wide track, between trees (Mare Way). Continue along the right-hand field edge to the signpost on the right, just beyond an Ordnance Survey Post and two concrete reservoirs.

Follow 'Wimpole 1' signpost and

6. Take the field edge to the right, to a marker post and turn right along a stony track between the hedge and the trees; keep direction down this farm track on the field edge with the trees to the right. Continue down the left-hand track at the fork, passing left of Cobb's Wood Farm, and follow this driveway left and right, to the road. Wimpole Home Farm was built as a model farm in 1796 by the 3rd Earl of Hardwicke. It keeps a range

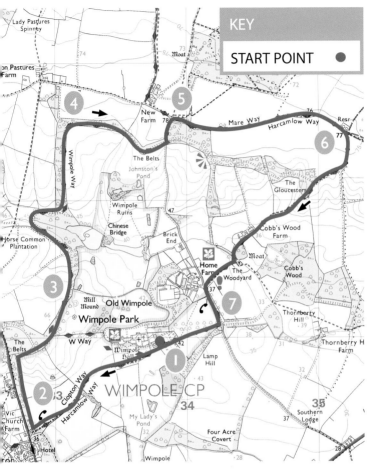

of farm animals in association with the Rare Breeds Survival Trust and displays a collection of vintage farm machinery and equipment.

7. Turn left, up to the Wimpole Park entrance and take the driveway right, back to the car park.

ABOUT THE AUTHOR

I was late on my feet apparently. I didn't walk until I was 16 months old and then only when I held on to a fold in the front of my dungarees (I have a photograph!). I still have a terrible sense of balance. I have since made up for this and over the last fifteen years have walked an estimated five thousand miles. I left school at 16 and never really found what I wanted to do for a living. Apart from a short period in my early 20s digging trenches with a JCB, I spent a long time trying to sell things: car spares, garage equipment, biscuits, custard powder, spanners, deodorant, antifreeze, oil, finance, socket sets, vacuum cleaners, insurance, audio systems, washing machines, extended guarantees, televisions, books and removals.

In 1999 I was made redundant and quickly found out that no one wanted to employ someone over 50. My wife and I already enjoyed walking; I am one of life's natural moaners and told her what I thought of some of the walking guides on offer. She very soon told me that if I thought I could do it any better I should get on with it.

The first three guides were finished just in time for the foot and mouth crisis and the ban on countryside activities. I eventually took the books to Peterborough and Oundle tourist information centres and tentatively asked if they were interested. They were; I had immediate orders for nearly two hundred copies of the books and have not stopped printing them since. There are now 83 books in the 'Walking Close to' series, spanning locations from East Anglia to Cumbria, Devon to Lincolnshire and Hampshire to the Midlands. The latest, two books covering the New Forest in Hampshire, were published in the spring of 2014. Total sales of the series are now in excess of 100,000 copies.

Image courtesy of John Hodder